Interviews with the Two Witnesses: Enoch and Elijah Speak

An Excerpt from Great Cloud of Witnesses Speak

Matthew Robert Payne

This book is copyrighted by Matthew Robert Payne. Copyright © 2017. All rights reserved.

No part of this publication may be reproduced, stored in a retrieval system or transmitted in any way by any means, electronic, mechanical, photocopy, recording, or otherwise, without the prior permission of the author except as provided by USA copyright law.

To sow into Matthew's writing ministry, to request a personal prophecy or life coaching, or to contact him, please visit http://personal-prophecy-today.com

Cover designed by akira007 at fiverr.com.

Edited by Lisa Thompson at www.writebylisa.com You can email Lisa at writebylisa@gmail.com for your editing needs.

Unless otherwise indicated, all Scripture is taken from the New King James Version. Copyright © 1982 by Thomas Nelson, Inc. Used by permission. All rights reserved.

New Living Translation (NLT). Holy Bible, New Living Translation, copyright © 1996, 2004, 2015 by Tyndale House Foundation. Used by permission of Tyndale House Publishers Inc., Carol Stream, Illinois 60188. All rights reserved.

Scripture quotations marked (NIV) are taken from the Holy Bible, New International Version®, NIV®. Copyright © 1973, 1978, 1984, 2011 by Biblica, Inc.™ Used by permission of Zondervan. All rights reserved worldwide. www.zondervan.com The "NIV" and "New International Version" are trademarks registered in the United States Patent and Trademark Office by Biblica, Inc.™

King James Version (KJV). Public Domain.

The opinions expressed by the author are not necessarily those of Revival Waves of Glory Books & Publishing.

Published by Revival Waves of Glory Books & Publishing PO Box 596| Litchfield, Illinois 62056 USA

Revival Waves of Glory Books & Publishing is committed to excellence in the publishing industry. Their website is www.revivalwavesofgloryministries.com Book design Copyright © 2017 by Revival Waves of Glory Books & Publishing. All rights reserved.

Paperback: 978-1-68411-401-6

Hardcover: 978-1-68411-402-3

Dedication

I want to dedicate this book to my dear friend, Lisa. Lisa is not only my editor, but she is a good friend to me and one of the people that I go to when I have an important decision to make in my life.

We all need people who can be honest with us and guide us and who have no fear of bringing correction or guidance to us when they feel that we are straying from God's path.

Acknowledgements

Father God

    I want to thank you for loving me, for leading me, and for making me into the person that I am today. Thank you for your Son, my best friend. Thank you for your Holy Spirit and Jesus.

Jesus Christ

    Thank you for being my friend for all of my life. I cannot thank you enough for all that you do in my life. I live to serve you and to do everything that you call me to do. I cannot imagine life without you. I thank you and the Holy Spirit each day for guiding me.

Bill Vincent

    I want to thank Bill Vincent, who produces my paperback books, my e-books, and my audio books. His company, Revival Waves of Glory Books & Publishing, has shown me great favor, and without him, I would be spending a lot more money to produce books. I give him my heartfelt thanks.

The Readers

    I want to thank my readers. I hope that you enjoy this book, and I hope that it encourages you to build a more obedient and trusting life on the rock of Jesus' teachings.

Ministry Supporters

    I want to thank all the people who have requested a prophecy from me, those who have requested a life-coaching session, and those who have requested your own message from an angel. I want to thank all those who have sown into my book-writing ministry. Without you, this book would not have been possible.

June and Bob Payne

    I want to thank my mother and father for all of their love and support.

Table of Contents

Dedication iv

Acknowledgements v

Introduction viii

An Interview with Enoch 1

An Interview with Elijah 14

I'd love to hear from you 35

Other Books by Matthew Robert Payne 37

About Matthew Robert Payne 40

INTRODUCTION

I first learned that the two witnesses were Enoch and Elijah and that they had bodies of flesh in heaven from a book on heavenly visits that Dr. D.G.S Dhinakaran wrote.[1] This little book recounted his visits to heaven. He has now passed on and is in heaven.

On one of his visits to heaven, he records that he met Elijah and Enoch. He records that their bodies shone like gold as they were the only people in heaven that he saw with bodies of flesh. When he met them, they asked Jesus if it was time for them to return to earth. Jesus told them that the time was not fulfilled and turned to the apostle and told him that they were the two witnesses of Revelation 11.

With that fact in mind, when I first met Elijah on earth in a vision, it was a big deal to me. I have now met him about ten times. I have met him as he walked with Enoch about five times also. Over the few times that we have met, I have begun to understand a little about him and his personality.

I had already been seeing saints for quite a number of years when, in 2014, Jesus asked me to record some videos and put them on YouTube with interviews of some saints that he collected for me. I interviewed nineteen saints and had the book transcribed into a book called *Great Cloud of Witnesses Speak*. As I made that book, I came under pretty vicious attacks from people that I considered friends, and this led to me removing the original videos from which the book came off YouTube. Thankfully, I recorded several more videos that remain on YouTube with interviews with other saints. They can be found on my channel Matthewrobertpayne1 under the playlist section.

---

[1] Dhinakaran, Dr. D.G.S. 2009. *An Insight Into Heaven*. Ampang, Malaysia. JN Cooray Publishing House. p. 79 and 80.

Yesterday, I was woken out of a sleep, and the Holy Spirit told me to take these two interviews out of the book and put together a short book with a new title. As I read the interviews, I made little edits and updated it slightly with information from books that I have written since. These books have been listed as resources. I pray that you enjoy what Elijah and Enoch have to say to the church today, years before they arrive.

AN INTERVIEW WITH ENOCH

Today's guest, as you read in the title, is Enoch, and he was said to be the seventh generation from Adam. He had such a fantastic relationship with God that God couldn't wait for him, and God just took him home. He didn't even die. Back in those days, saints lived for hundreds of years, so God grew impatient to be with him. He had such a tremendous relationship with Enoch, and he took him home early. You can read more about his story in Genesis 5:19-21. It's a great privilege to have him here. The first question that I have for Enoch follows.

How do you feel today about being here to speak to the whole world?

First of all, Matthew, it's an honor to be down here and to be part of this. It's always an honor to serve the living God. I am humbled that God would ask me to be a part of this project and to be part of this book. Being used by God is a great thing. Coming down to this earth and speaking to the people who are living here is a tremendous opportunity. Matthew, you have no idea how many thousands of people will read this book.

You seem to have no idea of how you will self-publish the book, and it's really in God's hands to make this a popular book. As you listen to us and bring our words to the people, you really have no idea how many people will read this and who it will affect, but I want you to know that we know. We know the people who will read it, and we know what we will say.

We know what effect our interviews with you will have on the people who listen to the videos and read the book. With all that being said, I want you to know that I love you, and I'm blessed to be in your house. I feel honored to have been here for half the night, having a conversation with you and your friend. It's a blessing that you would accept me and sit yourself down and do an interview with me.

What do you think is special to God?

Many people ask themselves, "What is really is special to God?" What I had going for me is that I loved God for who he was. I had an intimate relationship with God. Now, for those who are wondering about the Holy Spirit coming to Christians and about God speaking to people only when the Holy Spirit was here, you might wonder how I, the seventh from Adam, actually heard God speak and interacted with him. That's a good question, but God is able to speak to his people, and I was one of his people.

I had God in a special place in my heart, and he and I became closer and closer like you see children go round on a merry-go-round. They go round and round. You can push one of those self-propelled merry-go-rounds so that it spins really fast. The faster you push it, the more you will cling to it and the more you're stuck to the merry-go-round. This is similar to a ride at the fair where they spin it round so that you stick to the wall.

You can enter a certain momentum in your relationship with God where the closer you get to God and the more you draw closer to God, the more God draws closer to you. The more God draws closer to you, the more you draw closer to him. This holy momentum starts to operate so that you find yourself in a spinning vortex, going off the face of the earth into the heavens.

You find yourself walking and talking to angels and to God himself and having a deep and abiding relationship with God. Now, many saints through the history of the Bible had a relationship like that. Jacob saw Jacob's ladder; Joseph had a strong relationship with God, and so did Daniel. The Apostle Paul was caught up to heaven so many times that he hesitated to mention it in his books so that he would not appear prideful or have people think that they're not as spiritual as he is.

However, since the death of Christ and since the church was developed, many saints through history, contemporary saints, have had wonderful, life-giving relationships with God. A heart that's devoted to God is really special to him. It is amazing to enter into that holy vortex of relationship where you're continually drawing closer to God, and God is drawing closer to you.

When you're drawing closer to God, he'll draw closer to you like James 4:8 says. "Draw near to God and He will draw near to you." The closer you get to God, the better your relationship gets. The more you experience him and the more you get to know him, the more you understand the mind of God and the things of God.

The more you understand the mind of God and the things of God, the more you love him. The more you love God, the more you want to draw closer to him. The more you draw closer to him, the more he draws closer to you. So it goes until you're walking and talking with saints, and you're walking and talking with angels, and you're walking and talking with people in heaven because you're caught up to the heavens and because you live under an open heaven.

You will hear lots of talk about open heavens, and many people say that they're living under an open heaven, which is true. It truly is a blessing to live in a relationship where angels are manifesting in your life; Jesus is turning up in visions; you're walking through heaven; you're encountering Jesus on earth, and you're encountering angels.

You, too, might even encounter saints on earth. These are all things that come about when you have a wholesome relationship with God and when you're devoted to him 100 percent. The world can be really devious. The advertisements on television can be a powerful tool for Satan to misdirect people's attentions away from what's really important. The idea of spending time reading your

Bible, reading Christian books, and going to church might not be very appealing to the average person.

So many people think that prayer, the Christian life, and reading the Bible are boring. These are the most essential things that you need to develop an abiding and close relationship with God. The world has you duped. People like to talk about sports and politics, and they even like to talk about God.

However, the following subjects aren't popular with the average Christian:
- Giving to the poor
- Giving to God
- Self-denial
- Sacrifice and
- Suffering.

It's important to be close to God and to pursue him with everything that you have. This takes time and effort, but it's very rewarding.

What is one thing God said to you that impacted you?

It's hard to give just one answer. God said at one stage that I was a very good student. I was very impressed that he saw me with a hungry appetite for the things of God. He continued to show me different things and increasing levels of his glory and various paths of his wisdom. I was so encouraged when he told me that I was a good student. This certainly made me press in more and encouraged me in a greater measure.

He said that I had a wonderful disposition and a wonderful personality, which encouraged me. I think that some people can be very spiritual and can talk the talk and convince Christians that they're lovely people through their posts on Facebook.

However, when it comes to dealing with non-Christians, when it comes to dealing with the world, when it comes to dealing with the stranger in the streets and with the unlovely, these people can sometimes lack love and grace. They can pretend to be holy and spiritual, yet they might lack love. When God said that I had a lovely disposition, he was telling me that I was a wonderful person to others. That was a great compliment from him. He doesn't flatter people. We must understand that God doesn't say things just to puff you up and fill you with pride.

He actually sees the gold that is in you. He sees the precious parts of you, and he calls that out of you and tells you specific things that are good about you. Everyone is unique. Everyone is special. Everyone is chosen. God has special things to say to every person. He wants you to know that you're loved. He wants you to know that you're precious to him. He wants you to know that all the negative things that have been said about you were said to discourage you and were meant to pull you down, but God has a better report about you.

Even though you agree with some of the negative things said about you, God has a better way, and change is possible. A popular cliché says that "a leopard can't change its spots." It's sad that this is such a common saying because, through the blood of Jesus Christ and the resurrection power available through the Gospel of Jesus Christ and his grace, anything is possible, including any sort of change.

God wants you to know that even the negative things that have been said about you can be changed and turned around, and your turnaround can actually bring God glory.

What do you like about heaven?

Many of the saints have spoken widely about heaven in the book, <u>Great Cloud of Witnesses Speak</u>, and Matthew can remember some of what the saints have said. I want to talk about a different aspect of heaven in this question and use this question to lead into something else. You don't have to wait until you die to see heaven. It's all around you. In Luke 17:21, Jesus said that the "Kingdom of God is within you."

The Bible says that "We are . . . co-heirs with Christ" (Romans 8:17, NIV), and "he raised Christ from the dead and seated him at his right hand" (Ephesians 1:20, NIV). As a co-heir with Christ, you have the authority to also sit with Jesus on his throne. Jesus said in Revelation 3:21 that "to him who overcomes I will grant to sit with Me on My throne, as I also overcame and sat down with My Father on His throne." Are you an overcomer at the **end** of your life? Or are you an overcomer when you continue to overcome those things that come against you **during** your life?

Jesus said in Matthew 5:8 in the Beatitudes: "Blessed are the pure in heart, for they shall see God." Do you have to wait until you die to be pure in heart? Or can you be pure in heart and actually see God before you die? Jesus said in John 14:21 that anyone who knows his commandments and obeys them will be loved by him. The Father will love him, and Jesus will manifest himself to that person.

If you know the commandments of Jesus and are obeying them—love Jesus and love your brothers and sisters—do you have to wait for eternity to actually meet God and Jesus? Is it possible that, if you obey his commandments and if you love God and people, you can actually have Jesus manifest himself to you while you're living?

What I like about heaven is that you can see heaven, walk through heaven, and experience heaven while you're living. I want to encourage all of you to press into Jesus and to spend time with people who understand this. You can certainly meet people and interact with them who can show you how to have visions of heaven.

You can meet Jesus on earth. You can bring the Kingdom of heaven to earth. You can manifest healing and glory and all sorts of signs and wonders on earth. You don't have to wait until you die to go to heaven.

Many people are also wondering, did Enoch really write the book of Enoch? Many of the people who ask that question inherently understand already that I did write the book of Enoch.

But Matthew remembers the book of Enoch and even for him, it was way out there. Admittedly, he read it twenty years ago, but it seemed to be a bit supernatural and spiritual and above his head at the time. So many people who read it can't comprehend what it talks about and the things discussed in it. The information is rather advanced, so it's not something that everyone has to read or understand.

Yes, I did write it, but I was walking through heaven and experiencing heaven while I was a human on earth. I went to heaven so many times. I spent so much time with God and Jesus in heaven before Jesus was even born that they wanted me to stay in heaven forever.

It's as if you're a guest at a friend's house. You might go to your friend's house and spend time with their father and mother and their family. One day, the father and mother make a decision and say, "Can you just move in with us and live here?" It was the same with me. I was spending so much time in glory and in heaven that heaven just decided they weren't going to wait until I died. They were going to bring me to heaven right then.

I went to heaven in a human body, in a body of flesh, and now, I am not in a spiritual body in heaven. I have a human body in heaven because I will come back to earth one day to minister on earth.

Revelation 11 mentions two prophets who will come to earth and minister the grace of God and the saving Gospel of God and the judgements of God upon the earth. Those two prophets will shake up the earth and show the earth that there is a living God that you don't want to cross, and there is a loving God that you want to know. Those two and many other people will help harvest the face of the earth. Many people think that those two witnesses might be Moses and Elijah. Some people think it will be Elijah and John. I want to tell the people who are reading this book that I am one of the two witnesses mentioned in Revelation 11.

Even if achieve your destiny on earth, you go on to heaven and supersede your destiny here to do greater things and greater works there. For instance, years ago when Matthew recorded this, he worked with the Salvation Army and spent time serving coffee to the homeless and poor people. He will be one of the owners of a coffee shop in heaven. He will interact with the saints of heaven and make them coffee, sit down, talk to them, bless them, and interact with them.

Eventually, Matthew will be teaching people the things of God and how to access an open heaven and how to have an intimate relationship with Jesus through videos, books, and through the pulpit. When he gets to heaven, he will teach people the things of God and the greater wisdom and depths of God.

Some people assume that when they get to heaven, they will know everything there is to know. These people think that they will be like Christ. If everyone in heaven knew everything, how would anyone continue to learn? How would anyone change or be excited about new and interesting information? If everyone in heaven had equal knowledge, where would the leadership or authority be? Where would the levels of state or of society be that you have on earth? When you get to heaven, you don't know everything. In fact, when you get to heaven, you usually only know what you knew on earth.

If you spent all your time pursuing the things of the world and raising a family and buying houses and cars and living a lifestyle of the flesh, when you get to heaven, you'll have a lot to learn. Other people spend all their time and resources on the things of God and passionately pursue Jesus and have demonstrated an ability to be used powerfully by God on earth. They have known some of the secrets of God and known some of the hidden wisdom of God on earth and taught some of those truths. When these people who have pressed into God get to heaven, they won't be at the level of the person who lived a lifestyle of the flesh. They will stay at the level that they're at on earth. Then, they will be taken into more training and classes that will propel them forward like a slingshot, moving them into deeper levels.

God knows what excites people. He knows the unique characteristics and the personality of every single person. Some people in heaven will be happy to host dinner parties, and others will arrange flowers, and still others will be painters. Some people will be happy creating gardens for people in heaven where they can walk which will bring them joy. Some people will be happy looking after children and teaching them. Some people will be happy creating woodwork and all sorts of gifts that people can give each other. Some people will be glass workers who can work with fine glass and make beautiful creations as gifts. Whatever your talent, whatever your skill, you'll be doing that in heaven, blessing everyone and bringing joy to people.

No matter who you are, God knows you intimately. He knows what you love and what will make you supremely happy. Heaven is where everybody is incredibly happy.

What keys do you consider important for the Christian life?

I want to say that talk is cheap. Many people wear a cross around their neck or profess to be a Christian. Many people talk about wanting to save the world or their hate for injustice. Many people talk about how unhappy they are with their government. But the fact of the matter is that talk is cheap, and many people just talk about things instead of actually doing something to change the problem.

My advice for Christians and what I consider an important key for a Christian is to follow through on their words. If they truly are a Christian, why not be a little Christ to the world? That means that you don't backbite or gossip. That means that you don't steal from God but that you give to God. That's denying yourself, taking up your cross, and following Jesus.

If you want to call yourself a Christian and if you want to be known as a good Christian, you need to pursue being a little Christ on earth because that's what Christian means: "little Christ." You might want to demonstrate Jesus Christ to everyone you talk to and everyone you meet. Sometimes, it's a lot more important to be Jesus to a person than to preach Jesus to a person. So many zealous Christians try to make people repent and invite Jesus into their life and change their life.

But often, those same people preaching the message aren't loving people and aren't demonstrating the love of Jesus to others. Instead, you should be love to a person who needs love. For instance, instead of passing a homeless beggar as you walk down the street, actually stop and chat with him and buy him a drink or something to eat or even give him ten dollars.

When someone's talking to you who's very lonely and needy, listen to that person and don't make excuses to go off and talk to someone else because that person makes you uncomfortable. Instead, love the unlovely. Spend time with people who are really hurting and with people who really need your help. Talk is cheap. God wants a demonstration of both power and action in this world.

Matthew speaks at length about how to witness to people in your world in his book, *Influencing Your World for Christ*.

If everyone who marked "Christian" on a census actually obeyed Jesus and lived life the way that Jesus taught, the world would be a different place. You wouldn't need revival. You'd have revival. The keys to the Christian life that I suggest are to be real and not just talk about it. Like the Nike commercial says, "Just do it!"

What was the best lesson you learned in life?

I learned to pursue God with all my heart. I also pursued Jesus because I knew who Jesus was since I'd been to heaven and met him. Even though I lived before Jesus was sent to earth, I'd been to heaven and met the Holy Spirit, Jesus, and God. I knew what the plans of Jesus were to come to earth. When you're close to God, when you're intimately close to him, you know things and find out information that the average Christian doesn't know.

The best lesson that I had on earth was to actively pursue God with all that I had. I learned that not doing what God wanted me to do resulted in suffering and depression. From my depression, I learned to do what I felt God was leading me to do all the time. The more I did what God led me to do, the more ecstasy and joy I lived in and the more I lived in the heavenly realms.

The more I lived in the heavenly realms, the more I wanted to do what God wanted me to do every time he impressed something on my spirit. There's just this cycle of things getting better and better and better when you start to pursue God. I encourage you all to start to press in and go after these things like I did.

What message do you have for this generation?

I would like people in this generation to understand what patience is. Understand what it's like to wait thirty years to be trained up and have your character developed sufficiently to be in ministry. Understand that the longer you wait, the better your ministry might be and the more prepared you are to do great things for God. This world is a microwave age, an age where if a page doesn't load up on the internet within a couple of seconds, you don't even go to the page but click the second option on Google.

Impatient people live in today's day and age. Some people have developed tremendous patience, and God has helped them develop that patience. These people with great patience will do awesome things, but on the whole, many people are impatient. My message to your current generation is to be patient.

Take the time to do an excellent job of anything you put your hand to. Make the effort and use the time and resources you have to do the very best job that you can do. When you're a Christian, you're demonstrating Jesus Christ to the world. You're demonstrating something that is perfect to the world. The better you package that, the better you present what you're doing to the world, and the more perfection and excellence that you move in, the more glory God can get from what you do.

God's not interested in an average job. He's interested in excellence. With that being said, don't be too hard on yourself and think that you have to be perfect in everything that you do. Don't put too much pressure on yourself but certainly do the best job that you can with the available time, money, and resources that you have.

Another thing that I'd say for this generation is be prepared to experience heaven. Be prepared to start to prophesy. Matthew has books on how to prophesy and how to go to heaven.

Be prepared to start to hear from God. Be prepared to experience going on trips to heaven and meeting angels, Jesus, and saints. Be open. Open your ears. Increase in your hunger. Open your life to the supernatural. The more you open your life to the supernatural, the more you can be used and the more you can be blessed on this earth.

If there was one type of reader you had a special message for, what would that message be?

I have a message for the brokenhearted. Jesus is very close to the brokenhearted. Jesus cries when people cry on earth. When people are broken, it breaks the heart of Jesus. He wants you to know that he loves you and cares about you. He's seen your tears and heard your cries. He knows your anguish. He realizes that evil men do evil things and that bad situations happen. Satan controls a lot of what happens on earth.

If Jesus could prevent certain events in your life, he would, but men have free will. This free will prevents him from acting. Jesus wants you to know that if you're brokenhearted, he's in your corner. Just spend time in the Word of God, learning the principles and the promises of God. Start to claim those promises for your life. Start to pray for deliverance and pray for an end to the suffering. Start to have faith in God that he will intervene in your life.

You can read more about what saints have to say in *Great Cloud of Witnesses Speak* and *Great Cloud of Witnesses Speak: Old and New*. I enjoyed this conversation. God bless you.

An Interview with Elijah

Elijah was a prophet of God in the Old Testament. He was most famous for stopping the rain for three and a half years in Israel. He stopped the rain and brought the whole nation of Israel into judgement under a wicked king and caused a famine in Israel. He went to another country and hung out there with a widow. He confronted the three hundred or four hundred false prophets of King Ahab's wife, Jezebel. These were "witchcraft" prophets who served under Jezebel.

He confronted them and had them killed. He was famous for bringing down fire from God to burn the sacrifices, and fire fell from heaven. The king became angry and sent out a hundred men to take him into custody. Elijah said something like, "If I'm a prophet of God, let fire fall from heaven and consume you." The hundred men were immediately wiped out by fire.

Another hundred men came out, and he did the same to them. Then another hundred men came out, and the guy in charge said, "Please don't consume us with fire, but please come and see our king." He agreed and went to see the king. He had amazing power. I'm not sure if anyone else has called down fire on the earth before. I don't know if anyone else has ever taken out so many false prophets at a time before.

I'm not sure if anyone has ever stopped the rain for three and a half years since then. Elijah is very highly revered in Christian circles, especially because of the things he did and the determination and the authority that he walked in before the Holy Spirit came to all believers. I have prepared to interview first Enoch and now Elijah with much trepidation.

I have had a holy fear of approaching Elijah and sitting down and talking to him, but now, you have a bit of history on Elijah. If you didn't know much about him, this information is probably interesting and helpful. You can read more about him in 1 and 11 Kings. I'll start with the first question.

How do you feel today about being here to speak to the world, Elijah?

Matthew, there's nothing to fear from me. I will not do anything to you except impress you and make you fall even deeper in love with Jesus Christ. Jesus Christ is the living Savior of the world. A time is coming in the future when the Bible declares that "every knee (person) shall bow and confess that Jesus Christ is Lord." The Bible says **every man** "of those in heaven, and of those on earth, and of those under the earth, and that every tongue should confess that Jesus Christ is Lord" (Philippians 2:10-11).

Many people wonder where hell is. Well, the Bible tells us that it's below the earth. Even atheists and all the people who vehemently deny Jesus Christ will be put under such power and anointing by Jesus one day that they'll fall to their knees and say that Jesus Christ is Lord. I serve a risen Savior. Of course, when I lived, Jesus Christ wasn't alive on earth, but I knew his Father.

If you think that Jesus has authority, you should walk hand in hand with his Father, the Lord God of Israel. Many people ask who God is. My challenge to anyone reading this who doesn't believe in God is to ask God to show up in your life. If you have a sincere heart and if you want to know the truth, I challenge any reader or person reading this to ask God to reveal himself and show you beyond a shadow of a doubt that he loves you.

God will show up and will show you through miracles and through definite signs and wonders in your life that he exists. You won't be able to say that they are just a coincidence. If you ask him to reveal himself to you, he will. I served the Almighty God of Israel, the Almighty God who created heaven and earth and flung every star into orbit. He's still creating stars and has been since the day of creation. The universe is still expanding.

Your modern scientists on earth know that this is happening. The universe has no end, no end that can be seen. There's no end to God.

Before I even finish this interview, even more of the universe will have been created. I serve an Almighty God. I'm a prophet. I've proven myself. When I lived on earth, I had the authority of the King of Kings backing me. I have the authority of the Almighty God of heaven and earth, the Creator of all things behind me.

Some people wonder who the two witnesses will be that Revelation speaks about. Well, you've heard from Enoch in this book. You've heard him openly confess that he's one of the two witnesses, and I will say publicly here that I'm one of the two witnesses, too. Both of us are in the flesh in our bodies in heaven and have been seen by other people in the flesh in our bodies in heaven.

We're both awaiting a day that's coming in the not-too-distant future when we will come to earth and show the earth who's in charge and under whose authority we rule. We will show the skeptics what happens when you cross God. We will bring some of the governments in this world into account before a loving and just God, a God of justice and mercy. If they don't show mercy, we'll show God's justice to them.

For more about what we will do, you can read what Matthew believes in his book, *Optimistic Visions of Revelation*.

Mercy will only be dealt out to people who show mercy. If you don't show mercy, we'll show you God's hand of justice. We're ready! We're fired up! I'm ready right now. If it were God's timing right now, I'd appear and start my ministry on earth. If I have to hold back another twenty or thirty years or more, I'll be ready then as well.

We're ready to go! With all that being said, I'm happy to be here to talk to you and answer these questions.

What do you think is special to God?

God admires sincerity. He does not have a problem with a person who is sinning all of their life. God does not have an issue with a person who is broken and stuck in sin all of their life. God dealt with sin. Listen up! God dealt with sin. He crucified his Son, Jesus Christ. The precious Lamb of God came as a lamb; an innocent Lamb of God came to this earth, was laid down on an altar, and was slaughtered before the prince of the world.

He was slaughtered in front of the prince of this world, Satan, and crucified for the sons of God. He was crucified for you! Listen up! He was crucified for you, reader. All of the punishment, the entire wrath of God, was poured out on his Son, Jesus Christ, to redeem everybody. A lot of people have issues with sin when they should not have an issue with sin but have an issue with sincerity.

God loves someone who is sincere. If you love God and if you're sincerely pursuing after God, God loves that. He doesn't enjoy wishy-washy people. Now, God loves everybody, but he doesn't love a wishy-washy attitude in people. He doesn't like people who are two-faced. I'll repeat it. God loves everybody, but He doesn't like people who are two-faced. He doesn't like it when you confess that you're a Christian and that you love God, and then you walk past a homeless person without caring for them.

When they ask, "Do you have spare change?" you should not lie to the homeless person and say that you do not have any spare change when you have it in your wallet. He doesn't like you lying. He doesn't like you saying that you love God unless you hold yourself to this standard of righteousness. Many people deny a person who's starving and on the streets begging for your money. He doesn't like that two-faced attitude.

Many of you have walked past Jesus himself, and he has asked you, "Do you have any spare change?" On that great day of judgement, you'll be shown the video, and you'll know that Jesus asked you for money on that day. Now, Jesus paid the price for sin. Sin has been dealt with. His precious blood was poured out on Calvary for sin, but people will have to give an account for every action.

They will have to have their actions weighed in the balance one day. Sin is forgiven, but when God is giving out the rewards in heaven to his saints, you will know in that day that you walked past many people who were broken and that God wanted you to give them money. That's just one example of how people are two-faced.

People hate hypocrisy—saying one thing and doing another. The people who are of the world, those that you classify as non-Christians, hate hypocrites and two-faced people. You don't have to be a Christian to dislike two-faced people. God is different than how you think he is. He has emotions and feelings and is a personable God. He doesn't like it when you say one thing and do another.

He doesn't like it when you are a white-washed tomb. He doesn't like it when you are pretty on the outside and all nice and glossy and white when you go to church, but you are a gossiper who causes strife and division in your workplace. He doesn't like it when people know that you're a Christian but then you act un-Christian in front of all of them. He doesn't like that. Jesus died for everything, for every sin that you commit, but he doesn't like it when people are insincere. He doesn't like it when people are wishy-washy and two-faced.

Here are some things that are special to God since I've shared a couple of things that he doesn't like. As I've said, he likes sincerity. He likes people to be genuine. He likes those whose word is their honor.
Christians sometimes sing songs with lyrics similar to this: "I'll do anything. I'll lay down my life for you. Lord. It's only in your will that I am free." Or they might sing songs like, "My whole life

is surrendered to you, Lord." He likes it when you follow through on those promises. He likes it when you're led by the Holy Spirit to give five hundred dollars to a person who needs a deposit to move into a new apartment. When he puts it on your heart to give five hundred dollars to a person and you have the money in savings, he doesn't like you to say "no" to his Spirit.

He likes you to be genuine. You might sing a song with words similar to these, "My whole life is yours, and I only want to be in your will. I'll do anything to serve you, Lord." When he asks you for five hundred dollars, he wants you to remember that song that you were singing at church and gladly give your savings to that couple that will end up on the street with their children, living in a car because they can't afford a deposit for a place to live.

A time will soon come on the earth that things will grow very dark, and people will become very desperate. Things will start to get hard. If you think the Antichrist is scary, just wait until Enoch and I get here and start demonstrating God's authority on earth. You think a hundred soldiers being burnt to a crisp and then another hundred with the same fate is scary? You think that four hundred false prophets wiped out at the same time is scary? You wait until we control the weather patterns. You wait until we control all sorts of events on earth just by speaking them into being.

God wants you to be sincere and genuine. He wants you to be true to who you are. And who are you? As a Christian, Enoch shared, "You're a little Christ." He wants you to learn how to demonstrate Jesus to the world. He wants you to have the heart of Christ.

He wants you to have the mind of Christ. He wants you to walk in the Holy Spirit. In other words, he wants you to know what walking in the Holy Spirit is. Then, he wants you to do it. Galatians 5:16 says, "Walk in the Spirit, and you shall not fulfill the lust of the flesh." If everything you ever did was based on direction from the Holy Spirit, you'd never sin.

You don't stamp out sin by saying, "Don't do that." If you tell a child that they can't have chocolate, the child wants the chocolate even more. For example, a certain street might be filled with houses made of beautiful plate glass windows because gorgeous scenery surrounds the street. On this street is a sign that says, "Don't throw rocks at the houses. You'll break the glass." When a group of boys sees the sign, they pick up rocks and throw them at the glass houses. Why did they do that as soon as they saw the sign? Because the law propels us into sin. You will not stop sin in people's lives by telling them not to do something.

When you tell them not to do something, this motivates them to do it more. You have to show them the love and the grace of God and preach the grace of Jesus Christ to the world. God wants you to be love and to be genuine and sincere. These are some of the things that are special to God.

What is one thing or several things that God said to you that impacted you?

God told me that he was in my corner. Although he used different words, when God says that he's in your corner, it's sort of like a boxing term in the modern world. I'm just sharing that so that people know what it means. When a boxer is boxing, he has his coach and his trainer in his corner. Every time he comes back from a round of boxing, they're the ones who put the water in his mouth, wash him, and rub him down.

His coach talks right into his ear and tells him what his opponent is doing and how to counter that and how to fight back. The coach is there to support him and keep his boxer in the fight and give the boxer strategies to win the fight. The coach shows the boxer how to do what he's there to do, which is to win the fight. When God tells us that he's in our corner, he is saying that he's there for us and that he will back us all the way.

That was tremendously encouraging to me. When God said that he was in my corner and that he would support me, I really did need his support to do what I did.

A woman named Jezebel lived at the time. The term 'the Jezebel spirit,' which means a controlling person, comes from her name. She was the wife of the king who ruled the country and then, when she had wiped out all of the prophets, she said that she was going to kill me. She had a lot of authority and power in her name, which scared me. I ran off to a cave. You can read the rest of the story in your Bible in 1 Kings 19, but essentially, I wanted to give up. God took my ministry from me and let me come home to heaven.

When God said that he was going to back me up, I was really encouraged to do what I needed to do. He said many other great things to me. Anyone who's close to Jesus or to the Lord God Almighty can remember things God has said to them.

God told me that he admired my faith. It gives you even more faith when the God of the universe tells you that he admires your faith. I was just a simple person. Essentially, anyone who does great works is just a simple person.

People who think they are wise aren't wise. God really can't use people who are full of themselves and full of pride. It says in the Bible that 'knowledge puffs up' (1 Corinthians 8:1). In other words, the more knowledge that you accumulate in life, the more reason you have to become a proud person and think that you're better than you are. The people that shake and change nations are essentially simple people who have a simple concept and go forth in that idea. They are empowered by God himself. A modern person being used by God in this hour is Donald Trump although you might not agree with this.

People who have made great changes in the world are often simple people. I was essentially just a simple person. My power and my authority come from God Almighty. I'm not afraid to say that I'm no one. I'm just a person that you don't want to mess with because if you get my God angry, you'd better be fireproof.

I've already walked in this. People say that Elijah must be one of the two witnesses because the two witnesses will burn people. Scripture says that fire will come from their mouths and burn anyone that comes against them. They don't realize that this could actually be a prophetic word. I could speak over a whole nation and wipe them out with a prophetic word. Jeremiah 23:29 says, "Is not My word like a fire?" says the Lord, And like a hammer that breaks the rock in pieces?"

Everyone thinks that I will breathe fire out of my mouth because the passage mentions fire. They think that I will be some sort of fire-breathing dragon. I don't need to breathe fire, people. I don't need fire to burn people as they're running to kill me. Angels can deal with them. They might be hit by a stiff right arm that cuts off their heads from a sword that they can't even see.

When I walk the earth, hundreds and hundreds of snipers will be shooting bullets at my head. The bullets will veer off at right angles, and no one will be able to kill me. When I walk the earth, I'll practice translocation from country to country. I'll travel from country to country and just appear and do what I'm supposed to do in each country. Then, I'll disappear. I'll be in Australia in the morning and be in the United States two hours later. An hour after that, I'll be in the United Kingdom.

I'll be able to speak authoritatively to each of the major Western nations before lunch time, go out for a picnic with Jesus for lunch, and then come and see what nations have listened and bowed their knee to God. If not, I can bring calamity to those nations. It won't take three and a half years to make the nations of the world bow.

One thing Matthew knows and one thing that I know is that the whole Christian world seems to fear some things that they shouldn't really fear. They fear Satan. They fear demons. They fear false prophets. They fear the Antichrist. However, the only thing they don't seem to fear and revere is God himself. There's so much talk about the Antichrist. He is a pussy cat compared to what Enoch and I will be able to do. In fact, let it be said that the person who becomes the Antichrist will look like Jesus himself or even look like a peacemaker.

You might even find that this is a role reversal. Anyway, I won't say too much more on that. I'll just let you figure that out and argue it within your own mind or accept what I just said.

More on that topic is revealed in *Optimistic Visions of Revelation*, a book Matthew wrote years after the original recordings were made for this transcript.

What do you like about heaven?

How can you not like a place that is full of love, compassion, mercy, joy, peace, provision, lack of sickness, lack of fear, lack of worry, or lack of concern? How can you not love a place like that? Won't the world be a better place when all of those things disappear?

Let me talk about the future of the world.

Don't you look forward to a world that's like John Lennon's world in the song, *Imagine*? Imagine no borders. Imagine no possessions. Imagine no money. Imagine no countries fighting. Imagine a brotherhood of man.

Imagine everyone loving each other. Imagine that world! I challenge you to get over your worry about what Lennon said against heaven and hell and no religion. Get over those lyrics and go and listen to the song again. Take yourself away and just imagine if the world that John Lennon spoke about in his song happened on earth. Imagine peace, prosperity, no sickness, and no one earning or needing money.

Imagine if everyone could get things for free and if everyone could do exactly what they wanted to do. Imagine that every person who wants to write a film script could write a film script and see their film in movie theatres and on DVD. Imagine that every actor could have a role in a film or a play. Imagine that every writer who writes books could have their books read by thousands or millions of people.

Imagine every movie editor editing films. Imagine every book editor editing books and seeing their books go to the top of the most popular book list. (Remember, it's not about the highest sales because there's no monetary transactions involved.) Imagine whatever it is that you do and imagine excelling in that activity. Imagine finding what you were born to do and being able to do it with excellence. Can you imagine that world? Let's forget about heaven for a moment, and let's think about bringing heaven to earth.

Imagine a world with no injustice, no crime, no drugs, no confusion, no pain, and no sickness. If the world becomes that good, you wouldn't want to leave it. You'd want to live there forever. But one entity has to disappear from that earth for that to happen. In this way, men won't be ruled by evil. Satan will have to leave for a time.

Then, men and women will be retrained on how to love and not be envious, jealous, selfish, or filled with any other evil trait. You know, about five years ago, Matthew came across a revelation that if you removed selfishness from the world, most of the problems of the world could be solved. Injustice only happens because people are selfish. You want to change the world? Give two dollars every time someone asks you for your spare change.

Selfishness is the only thing that stops people from giving. Selfishness is the fear of lack. I serve a mega-abundant God of provision. Don't give your money to people or to God to get a hundredfold return. Give your money to people and to God because you love people and you love God.

Give money to people who are poor and to ministries because you love God and you want to do mighty works in the world through supporting ministries. If you give out of love, God will return it to you. He might return the same as what you gave or a tenfold or even a hundredfold return, but if your motivation for giving is to receive, you won't get it back.

People have to learn not to be selfish. We won't bring change to this world until the Christians change this world. None of the messages that Matthew has done in the *Great Cloud of Witnesses Speak* have been like this. He had real reason to fear interviewing me. He has met God himself and met Jesus many times. He felt like he was going to meet God on earth, and Matthew's a little scared of God.

Everyone should be in love with God but have a little fear, respect, and honor toward him. If selfishness were taken from the earth and from the church, this world would be transformed.

If you want to make an impact in this world, if you want to see the church make an impact in this world, you need to change your behaviors now and be part of the solution.

God wants you to know that he loves you. He wants you to know him. He doesn't want you to know **about** him. He doesn't want you to pray to him and think you know about him. He wants you to actually **know** him. He wants to **know** you. In the ancient times, to 'know' a woman was to have sexual intercourse with her. Genesis 4:1 says that Adam knew Eve and that they bore a son. One day, Jesus will say, "Depart from Me, I never knew you," according to Matthew 7:23. God is searching for an intimate relationship with everyone.

God wants you to be part of his army. Everyone can be involved in bringing harvest to this world. Everyone has a purpose. Everyone can do something to change this world. God wants you to know and love him. He wants you to love him for who he is, not for what you can get from him. God wants you to know who you are, know what you're designed for, and know what you're created for. He wants you to do those things with excellence.

Matthew has a book about this called *Finding Your Purpose in Christ*.

God wants you to succeed in the destiny that he has planned for you. He wants you to know him. He doesn't want you to fear him. Matthew understands about fear because he had an angry and violent father. He has this fear in his heart, but God doesn't want you to fear him. He wants you to know him and to love him. Jesus paid a big penalty, a big price. He was beaten to a pulp and hung naked on a cross, on a tree—for you and for me.

Jesus' death on the cross paid for our salvation. All of our sins were covered by Jesus. All of your sins in the future are covered by him. He loves you and delights in you. Won't you come to him? Won't you confess your sin? Won't you confess your struggles? Won't you come to the table with open hands and say, "I am lacking, Jesus. Please help me find my destiny and my purpose. Please help me fall in love with you. Please help me to live in a relationship with you that's so intimate that I can be used to change my generation."

He's looking for people who want to serve him. The harvest is ripe. It's ready and mature. The world is ready to be harvested. As times become harder and darker, people will become more desperate. Money, food, and peace will grow scarce. People will want food, comfort, love, peace, and joy. You can be the source of that for them.

Don't you want to move into a relationship that is an abiding one, a relationship where Jesus is the vine and you're the branch? Wouldn't you like to have a big strong branch full of fruit so that people who are hungry can come and just take the fruit from the branch that they need, according to Psalm 1:3 and Jeremiah 17:7-8?

If a person needs a hundred dollars, you have a hundred dollars for him. If a person needs two hours just for you to listen and to weep on your shoulder, you have the time and the resources to be able to help them with their pain. If people need to be taught something in the Bible, you have the skill and the wisdom to teach them what they need in the Bible. If a person needs a personal assistant, you have an hour or five hours a week to be their personal assistant.

How would you like to have the money to finance missionaries who are saving hundreds of people in other nations? What if all of those hundreds and thousands of people who were saved though your finances came to you in heaven and thanked you for the rest of eternity for saving their lives? How would you like to have the answer to every person's question? Even if you didn't have the answer when they asked, how would you like to have access to the Holy Spirit so that he could speak the answers through you?

How would you like to be that branch full of fruit? To be full of love, joy, peace, patience, self-control, gentleness, mercy, kindness, and more! Not just the fruit of the Spirit but full of wisdom with answers to their problems and solutions for the needs of the people. Sure, you need the fruit of the Spirit to minister to all people, but the fruit isn't just fruit of the Spirit. How would you like to be a beautiful tree planted by the waters where the roots of your life go into the abundant streams of the living water of the Holy Spirit?

How would you like the birds of the air to come and flock and roost in your branches? That is, for tired and hungry people to come and take fruit from your tree and sit in the shade underneath your branches and your leaves on a hot day? How would you like to be someone who can make anything that you turn your hand to prosper? How would you like to be the answer to everybody's problems? How would you like to be that person?

How would you like to be the tree (person) described in the passage below?

Psalm 1:1-3 (NLT)

"Oh, the joys of those who do not follow the advice of the wicked, or stand around with sinners, or join in with mockers. But they delight in the law of the Lord, meditating on it day and night. They are like trees planted along the riverbank, bearing fruit each season. Their leaves never wither, and they prosper in all they do."

How would you like to be that person? The first couple of verses talk about what you need to do to be that person and the third verse talks about who you become when you do those things. Do you know that everything has a cost? Everything has a reason. There's a price for everything, a price to be paid. You don't become the very best in the world by luck. You don't get to be the best in the world just by chance. You get it with a lot of practice and determination.

I'm not sure of what it's like where you live, but Matthew knows a couple of sons of billionaires, and they are not performing like their fathers. They're rich and wealthy, but they're not the men that their fathers who built the empires were. No matter what man achieves on earth, he has to have a son who can handle and manage the fortune. You don't become excellent by sitting around all day, complaining and wishing that things were better for yourself. You excel by applying yourself. You become excellent at prophecy by practice. You become excellent at carrying the voice of God by doing it many, many times.

You become so proficient at carrying the voice of God that you could do a book like this because of many, many hours of practice over thousands of times. It's incredibly easy for us to sit in Matthew's lounge room and for Matthew to record what we have to say. He's been prophesying for years, and God has spoken through him. The only difference is that, now, I'm speaking through him. Many of you will wonder what I have to say next, and Matthew doesn't even know.

God is the boss. It doesn't look like God is in control of this world. It doesn't look like he has control, but times are changing. Things will change. A generation of Christians is being born who will rise up. This includes a generation of young people and older people, those who are Matthew's age, who will do great things. A generation of even older people will also rock this world.

Real people will change this world. As the darkness pours in, as the darkness gets darker, as situations and people start to become desperate, the manifest presence of God will increase on a whole army of believers. Those believers will go around the whole world and set the whole world alight with healing, signs, and wonders. See Isaiah 60:1-6.

People might challenge this book of Matthew's. Religious people will say, "This isn't happening." Every prophet had their mockers. Not many prophets lived to a ripe old age in the Bible. Many prophets lost their lives because of their message. Religious people have always disagreed with the things of God.

Religious people don't change the world. People who are stuck and bound by a set of rules don't change anything. We already addressed this. Don't throw rocks at the glass house. Kids still pick up rocks and throw them. Rules aren't the answer. Love is the answer. If you want to change the world, love. Think of the world. Just imagine a world like the world I described.

Imagine walking into that world. Before heaven comes to earth, heaven will exist in pockets of the earth. Christians will be charge in certain towns and cities. All the people who aren't Christians in the city will be blessed by how the city is run. Jesus and God are very merciful. They allow everyone to have free will and to make a choice.

Jesus and the Father will not force anyone to become a Christian, and neither should you! A person shouldn't be pressured or motivated by guilt into becoming a Christian. They should see you as so dynamic and beautiful that they want to become like you. The way to preach Christ is to shut your mouth about them being a sinner. Instead, just be Jesus to them until they can't cope with it anymore.

They might say, "What makes you different? Why are you so happy? I know what's going on in your life, and a lot of tragedy is happening right now. How do you stay so positive?" Things will change.

Millions of people will rise up and start to shine with the glory of God on their skin. They will walk around like mini suns. These people will be anointed to heal. They will have answers and solutions to people's problems. They will be able to direct people to money. They will direct people about how to get off the streets. A whole lot of them will be living Psalms 1:1-3. Millions of them will be alive, and they will save the world. The whole world isn't just waiting for me and Enoch to come.

We have a vital job to do, and we will do that job. We will exercise love, justice, and mercy. Those who aren't merciful will see God's wrath and justice. Those with good hearts will see God's love coming through us. We have a very special assignment in the world.

Matthew's read about a hundred accounts of people who've written about our job. He's never seen anyone write great details about what we will do. They can't even agree on who we are. What sort of experts are they? All it takes is someone asking Jesus who we are, and you'll know if they are speaking the voice of Jesus. You can trust Jesus. Why not just ask him? The whole world still wonders who wrote the book of Hebrews, but they're supposed to be sheep that can hear Jesus' voice.

He says in the parable of the good shepherd in John 10, " the sheep hear his voice; and he calls his own sheep by name and leads them out" (v. 3). You should be able to hear Jesus' voice. When Matthew wondered about the writer of Hebrews, he just asked Jesus, "Did Paul write Hebrews?" Jesus answered, "Yes." When Joseph Prince preaches, he says, "Now, when Paul wrote this . . . . " and he's quoting from Hebrews.

He doesn't even tell his audience, "Hey, guess what? Paul wrote Hebrews." He just quotes from it. When you have a living, talking, dynamic relationship with Jesus, you can know all things. The mind of Christ is really having Jesus in your mind. Can you imagine that? Can you imagine having peace in the midst of calamity? Can you imagine being in a boat that's going to sink in the middle of the storm in a turbulent ocean? Can you imagine being Jesus in that boat? Can you imagine sailing a stormy sea yourself? Can you imagine turning a hurricane around?

Can you imagine turning an ocean to blood like we will do? All it takes is faith. Jesus said that all it takes is a mustard seed of faith.

Matthew thought that I would discuss heaven, but we did not stay on that topic. Now, we're coming back to the questions. Matthew didn't realize what subjects we would cover, but you needed to know what I just shared so that we could achieve our purpose.

When this question was covered in <u>Great Cloud of Witnesses Speak</u>, all of the nineteen saints answered the question about heaven except me.

What keys do you consider important for the Christian life?

One key I would suggest is getting to really know Jesus. Get to really know him.

When you start to hear from God and Jesus, ask questions. When you read something in the Bible that you want an answer to, just ask Jesus what the answer is. The Scriptures say in 1 John 2:27 that you don't need a teacher. The anointing is with you to teach you. The Holy Spirit is there to teach you. Ask Jesus, and he'll bring the voice of Jesus to you through the Holy Spirit.

What were the best lessons you learned in life?

One of the best lessons I learned in life was to hear God's voice and to obey it. I learned not to doubt what God said to do. When I heard it, I acted on it. This is a lesson every Christian should learn.

It took a lot of faith to get the courage to do what I did to the nation of Israel. To get to that level of faith, I had to have confidence when I heard God's voice. The only way to be confident in the voice of God is to hear God tell you to do things, for you to do them, and for them to work out perfectly for you.

The best lesson I learned in life was to build my faith and confidence in God's voice by doing hundreds of things that he told me to do. By obeying God, you find out that he is really smart. He is really wise, so it is best to do what he tells you to do.

For example, imagine that an architect designed a building and submitted the plans to the city council for approval. If the builders build the building according to the architect's plans, then the building will be approved. If the builders started building the way they wanted and ignored what the architect said, the architect might tell the city council that the builders were taking shortcuts. The city council would close down the building site. The builder would have to make sure he was at least fooling the architect into thinking that he was building correctly according to the plans.

Why are you trying to build a life in this world without listening to your architect as a Christian?

Jesus stated quite clearly in the Sermon on the Mount in Matthew 5 to 7 how to live the proper Christian life. At the end of the sermon in Matthew 7:26-27, he said, "But everyone who hears these sayings of Mine, and does not do them, will be like a foolish man who built his house on the sand: and the rain descended, the floods came, and the winds blew and beat on that house; and it fell. And great was its fall."

To further analyze what Jesus said, people who do not hear and apply the words that he taught or any of the instructions that he gave in the Gospels are building a life that is willingly ignoring the architect's plans. When the storms and the floods come, his house will collapse because it is built on the wrong foundation.

If you are not building on the right foundation, your house will fall flat. If you are worried about the darkness and the trouble coming to the world, you have to ask yourself, do you know the fifty commands of Jesus in the Gospels, and are you doing them? Are you building your house on the rock of Christ's teaching? Or are you building your house on sand? In other words, do you know what Jesus said to do and are you refusing to do it?

If you knew what Jesus said to do and if you're not doing it, when hard times come to this world, you will suffer. There's plenty of time now to correct that and start to live the way Jesus taught before it's too late.

What message do you have for this generation?

I want you to know that time is short. I'm not saying that it will be ten or twenty or even thirty years. I'm not even saying that it will be forty years. Hundreds of so-called experts on the book of Revelation give dates and times and offer so many opinions. Many people have apparently heard from God about when Jesus is coming back. If I give you a date, it will just confuse you because it won't line up with something that someone else said.

Some supposed expert or someone who apparently heard from God or someone who saw it in a vision will have their opinion. What I will say is this, and I'll repeat it. Time is short. This is not the time to be building your house on the sand. This is the time to be listening to and obeying Jesus. In the days and years to come, you want to be able to hear Jesus' voice.

Moses said that he wished that all men were prophets. Paul said that we're to desire the best gifts. He went on to say that prophecy is the best gift in 1 Corinthians 14. He also went on to say that we should covet the gift of prophecy. In other words, prophecy is the ability to hear God speak and to be able to speak that word to other people if need be. You need to be able to hear God speak. You don't need to run to a prophet to hear God speak. You need to be able to hear from him yourself. You need to know what Jesus taught and know his commandments.

Start to obey his commandments and start to obey everything he tells you to do. You need to really practice obeying Jesus, You have to be able to discern between your mind's thoughts and when Jesus is talking. You have to be very confident and have faith and discernment when Jesus is talking. You need the ability to tell when Jesus is talking because a time will come when you won't be allowed to walk down a certain street.

You will have to ask Jesus which way to go. For example, he'll tell you, "Turn around. Go three streets down. On your left, go to Ginger Street and follow that until you reach a mountain top. On the top of the mountain, sit under the highest tree, and someone will come and meet you." You need to be able to do that. If you continue on the street, you'll be killed. Things will be desperate in times to come.

You have to be able to hear from Jesus, and everyone who's a Christian can hear from Jesus if they try.

If there was one type of reader you had a special message for, what would that message be?

My message here has been pretty plain and clear. I've said a lot of things, and you notice that I become excited and speak with authority. I'm a lot calmer now, but I still want you to pursue and know Jesus. I don't want you to know **about** him. I want you to be able to write a hundred pages of things Jesus has told you. All of you can get a notepad or a journal and start to keep a journal.

Pray to Jesus in the journal. Write down your prayers and then listen to Jesus and write down what he says. I hope that you've been blessed by what I've had to say.

I'D LOVE TO HEAR FROM YOU

One of the ways that you can bless me as a writer is by writing an honest and candid review of my book on Amazon. I always read the reviews of my books, and I would love to hear what you have to say about this one.

Before I buy a book, I read the reviews first. You can make an informed decision about a book when you have read enough honest reviews from readers. One way to help me sell this book and to give me positive feedback is by writing a review for me. It doesn't cost you a thing but helps me and the future readers of this book enormously.

If you would like to sow money into a portion of a book or even into an entire book, please visit my website and ask me what projects I am working on.

To read my blog, request a life-coaching session, request your own personal prophecy, request a visit to heaven, or to receive a personal message from your angel, you can also visit my website at http://personal-prophecy-today.com All of the funds raised through my ministry website will go toward the books that I write and self-publish. Feel free to sow money into my book-publishing ministry as the Holy Spirit leads you.

To write to me about this book or to share any other thoughts, please feel free to contact me at my personal email address at survivors.sanctuary@gmail.com

You can also friend request me on Facebook at Matthew Robert Payne. Please send me a message if we have no friends in common as a lot of scammers now send me friend requests.

You can also do me a huge favor and share this book on

Facebook as a recommended book to read. This will help me and other readers.

OTHER BOOKS BY MATTHEW ROBERT PAYNE

The Prophetic Supernatural Experience

Prophetic Evangelism Made Simple

Your Identity in Christ

His Redeeming Love- A Memoir

Writing and Self-Publishing Christian Nonfiction

Coping with your Pain and Suffering

Living for Eternity

Jesus Speaking Today

Great Cloud of Witnesses Speak

My Radical Encounters with Angels

Finding Intimacy with Jesus Made Simple

My Radical Encounters with Angels- Book Two

A Beginner's Guide to the Prophetic

Michael Jackson Speaks from Heaven

7 Keys to Intimacy with Jesus

Conversations with God: Book 1

Optimistic Visions of Revelation

Conversations with God: Book 2

Finding Your Purpose in Christ

Influencing your World for Christ: Practical Everyday Evangelism

Deep Calls unto Deep: Answering Questions on the Prophetic

My Visits to the Galactic Council of Heaven

The Parables of Jesus Made Simple: Updated and Expanded Edition

Great Cloud of Witnesses Speak: Old and New

Walking under an Open Heaven

A Message from My Angel

You can find my published books on my Amazon author page here: http://tinyurl.com/jq3h893

Upcoming Books

Gaining Freedom from Sex Addictions: Breaking Free of Pornography and Prostitutes

Mary Magdalene Speaks from Heaven: A Divine Revelation

About Matthew Robert Payne

Matthew was raised in a Baptist church and was led to the Lord at the tender age of eight. He has experienced some pain and darkness in his life, which has given him a deep compassion and love for all people.

Today, he runs a Facebook group called "Open Heavens and Intimacy with Jesus." Matthew has a commission from the Lord to train up prophets and to mentor others in the Christian faith. He does this through his Facebook posts and by writing relevant books on the Christian faith.

God has commissioned him to write at least fifty books in his life, and he spends his days writing and earning the money to self-publish. You can support him by donating money at http://personal-prophecy-today.com or by requesting any of his other services available through his ministry website.

It is Matthew's prayer that this book has blessed you, and he hopes it will lead you into a deeper and more intimate relationship with God.

www.ingramcontent.com/pod-product-compliance
Lightning Source LLC
LaVergne TN
LVHW021740060526
838200LV00052B/3388